Wonders of the Pond

Written by Francene Sabin
Illustrated by Leigh Grant

Troll Associates

Library of Congress Cataloging in Publication Data

Sabin, Francene.
    Wonders of the pond.

    Summary: Describes the many varieties of plants
and animals that live in a pond.
    1. Pond ecology—Juvenile literature.
[1. Pond ecology.   2. Ecology]   I. Grant, Leigh.
II. Title.
QH541.5.P63S23   574.5′26322   81-7407
ISBN 0-89375-576-1   AACR2
ISBN 0-89375-577-X (pbk.)

It is a warm summer day. A gentle breeze moves through the trees. It makes small ripples across the pond. A bullfrog, sunning itself on a lily pad, croaks a loud song.

This is the world of the pond, where many special plants and animals make their homes.

A family of ducks waddles into the water. The mother leads four ducklings in a line close to the shore. All at once, the mother tips forward. Only her tail shows above the water.

The mother duck eats weeds that grow in the water.
These green plants are called *pondweed*. Tiny fish and snails
hide in the pondweed. It shelters them from big fish, ducks,
and other hunters.

Some fish swim along the muddy floor of the pond, hunting for food. They are called *bottom feeders*. One kind of bottom feeder is the sucker. The sucker's mouth is at the lower part of its face. The sucker feeds by taking in the tiny plants and animals, which are in the mud at the bottom of the pond.

The bottom of a pond is a very busy place. Many things grow and live there. Plants grow in every part of the pond. That is because a pond is not very deep. Sunlight can touch every part of the pond, from top to bottom. Plants need this sunlight to grow.

Every plant and animal plays an important part in the life of the pond. Even after a plant dies, it is used. It breaks down and makes the mud into good soil, where more plants will grow. Dead plants also are food for the tiny living things in the water. One of these tiny animals is the *amoeba* (uh-*mee*-bah).

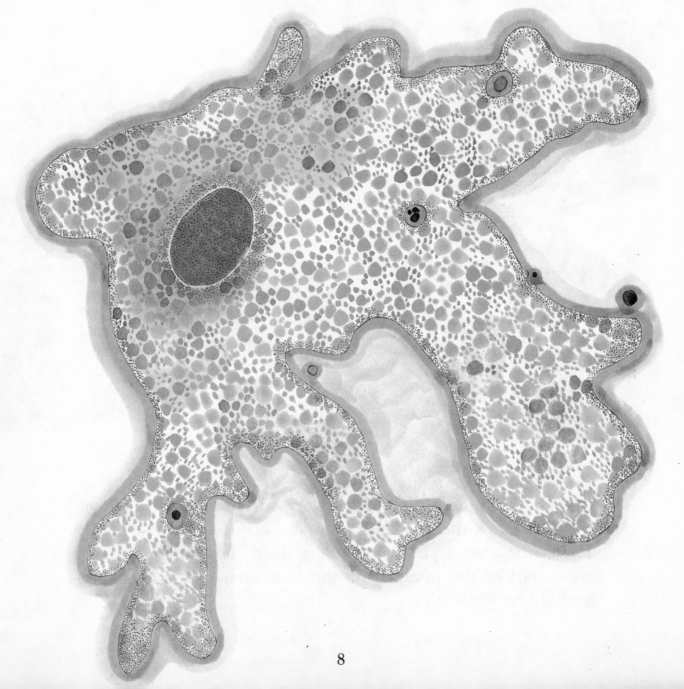

An amoeba is so small, it can only be seen under a microscope. It can have any shape. The amoeba can stretch out, long and thin. Or it can curl up into a round blob.

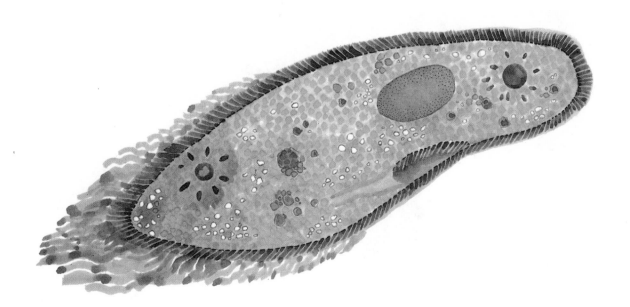

There are other animals the size of an amoeba in the pond. The *paramecium* (par-uh-*mee*-see-um) is one kind. It looks like a shoe with little hairs all over it. It swims by waving those hairs.

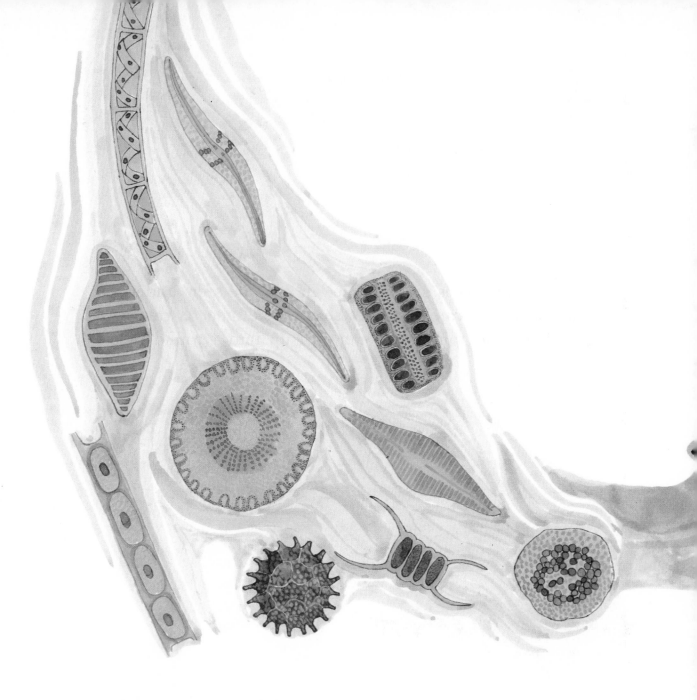

There are tiny living things in the pond that are not animals. They are plants called *algae* (*al*-jee). Under the microscope, they look like strings of beads, needles, flowers, and many other things.

The tiny plants and animals in the pond are food for bigger animals, such as water mites. Water mites look like their cousins, the land spiders. Water mites breathe air, but they can stay under the water for as long as an hour. Many water mites are eaten by fish that live in the pond.

Worms are also part of the life of a pond. There are *flatworms* that slide along the muddy bottom. And there are *roundworms* that move by whipping themselves back and forth in the water.

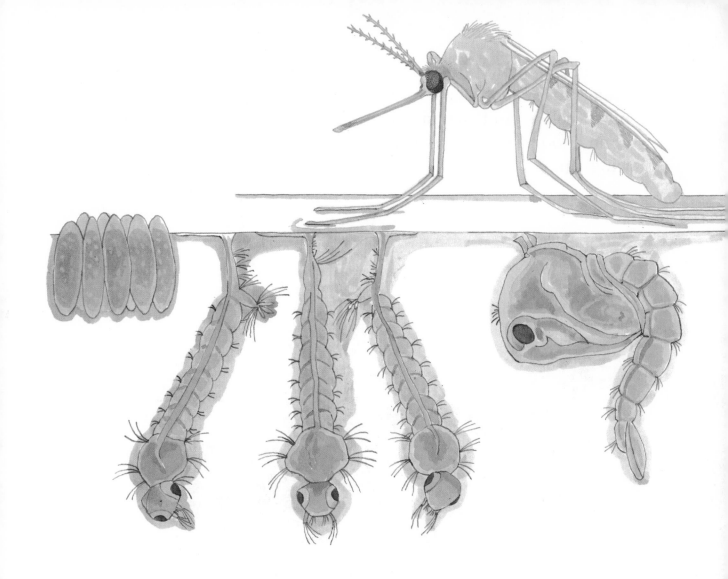

Many insects live near the pond, too. Mosquitoes lay their eggs at the edge of the water. The tiny eggs are laid early in the spring and hatch when the weather is warm. When they hatch, they look like little worms, floating on top of the water. A mosquito changes many times before it is a fully grown insect with wings.

The dragonfly is a very beautiful pond insect. It has a long, narrow body and four thin wings. Dragonflies come in many colors, and they are large insects. A dragonfly can be almost four inches, or ten centimeters, wide, from wing tip to wing tip.

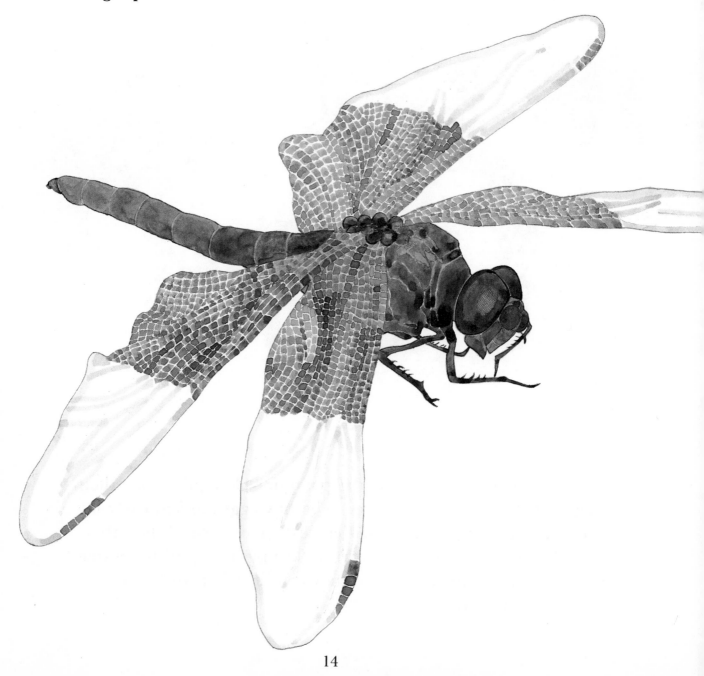

Dragonfly eggs are laid on the pond water or on the plants that grow in the pond. They hatch into little insects called *nymphs*. These nymphs look like very small beetles. Dragonfly nymphs live at the bottom of the pond for a year or longer.

When nymphs are ready to become dragonflies, they climb up a plant to the air. Once the nymph is out of the water, its skin splits open. Out comes a dragonfly. It spreads its wings and flies away.

There are hundreds of different kinds of insects at the pond. *Water striders* seem to skate over the top of the pond. *Backswimmers,* shaped like a boat, move around with legs like paddles. And there are flies, beetles, moths, plus many more.

Where the pond is shallow, shrimp and crayfish live. To swim, the shrimp turn onto their sides and wave their legs.

Crayfish look like small lobsters. Their shells are grayish-brown and hard. The crayfish has five pairs of legs. The pair in front are claws, used to catch and hold small fish, insects, or plants.

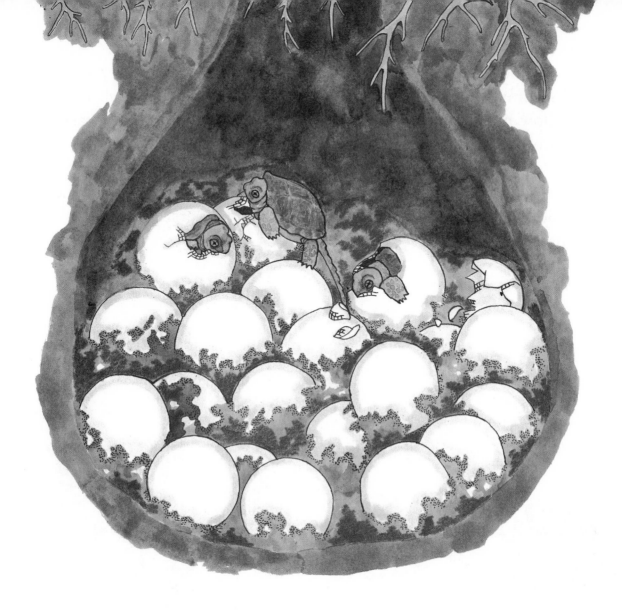

Snapping turtles are the biggest animals in the pond. They can grow to be two feet, or sixty centimeters, long and weigh more than forty pounds, or eighteen kilograms. Snapping turtles spend the winter in the mud at the bottom of the pond. In spring, they come out and dig a hole in the ground near the pond. This is where they lay their eggs. The eggs hatch into tiny turtles in about three months.

There is a creature of the pond that looks like a very small dinosaur. It's the salamander. Salamanders can be black with yellow marks, brown with blue spots, or bright red with black spots.

Some salamanders do not have lungs. They breathe through their skin! But they must keep their skin wet to be able to breathe and stay alive. All salamanders eat worms, insects, and snails.

Frogs start life as eggs laid in the pond. After a few days, they hatch into tadpoles, little swimmers that look like fish. It takes two years for a tadpole to become a bullfrog.

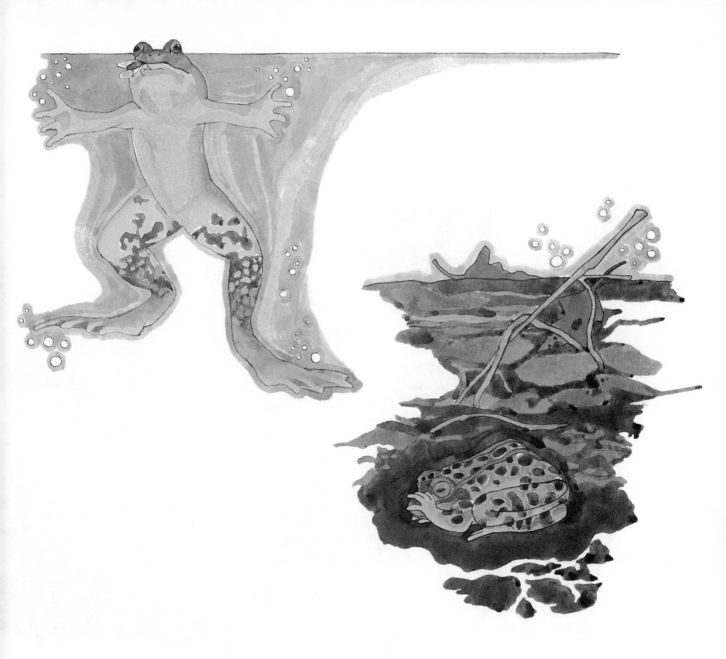

Frogs spend all their lives in or near the pond. They sit in the sun and catch insects flying by. Or they dive into the water to catch small fish. When winter covers the pond with ice, the frogs find a warm, dark place beneath the ground or deep in the pond. There they sleep until spring.

Snakes live near the edge of the pond, where the water is not deep. They eat tadpoles and frogs, salamanders, fish, and worms. Like frogs, snakes sleep through the winter.

Fish of many different sizes and shapes live in the pond. The *pumpkinseed sunfish* is very colorful. It is blue, green, and orange. Near each eye, this fish has a bright red spot.

There are many small fish in the pond. Little minnows dart here and there through the plants. The pickerel hides under a lily pad, waiting for a small fish to swim by. The pickerel is hard to see in the water. It is green and golden brown. It looks like the plants around it. A minnow glides by. The larger fish darts forward and catches it with sharp teeth.

Many birds come to the pond. The red-winged blackbird builds a nest around cattails in the pond or on a bush nearby. It lays three or four eggs in the nest. In two weeks, the eggs hatch. Mother and father blackbird feed the baby birds insects from the pond.

The little marsh wren and the great blue heron stop at the pond when they fly south in the autumn. They visit again on their way north in the spring.

How did the world of this pond begin? It all began as the work of one animal—the beaver.

Beavers make ponds. They do this by building a dam across a stream. The beaver cuts down trees with its strong teeth. Then it drags the logs into the water and builds its house with them. The dam holds back the water of the stream, and it collects. Finally, a pond is born.

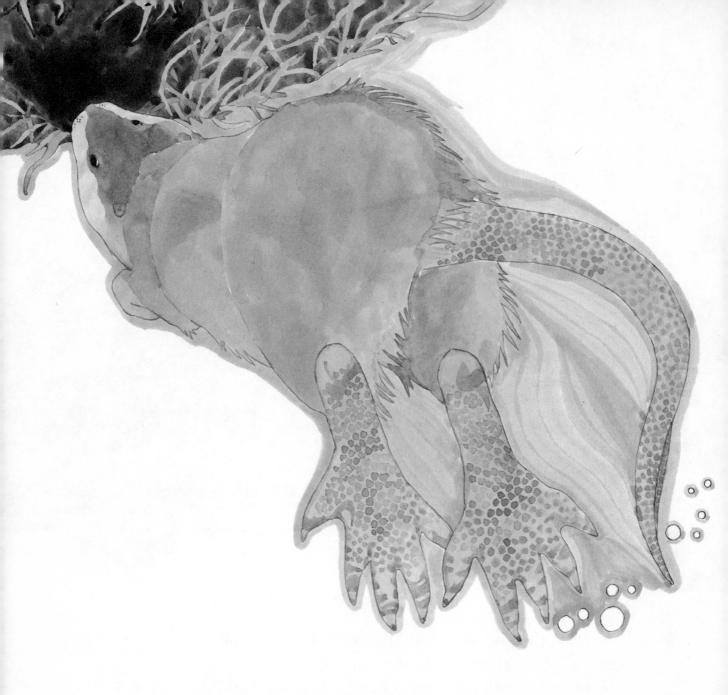

Like the beaver, the muskrat builds a house under the water. The house is made of mud, reeds, and cattails. The muskrat, a fine swimmer, uses its partly webbed feet like paddles.

Spring and summer are times of great activity at the pond. When cold weather comes, life slows down. The green plants at the pond's edge turn brown and die. Birds fly away to warmer places. Some animals go to sleep in their homes under the water. The fish swim slowly all winter long.

But spring will come again, bringing warm weather. Once more, the pond becomes a busy place. The birds return. The animals come out of their winter sleeping places. The plants are green again. Nature has awakened the pond, and it is bursting with life!

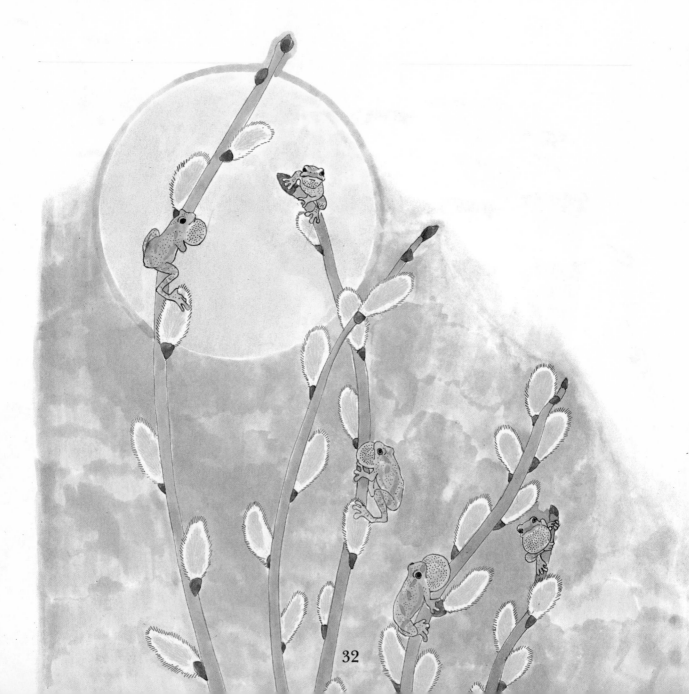